Y0-BGF-973

BOOKS AUTHORED OR CO-AUTHORED
BY ELAINE CANNON

Elaine Cannon

Bookcraft
Salt Lake City, Utah

Library of Congress Catalog Card Number: 97-74879
ISBN 1-57008-340-1

First Printing, 1997

Printed in the United States of America

For unto you
is born this day
in the city of David
a Saviour,
which is Christ the Lord.
—Luke 2:11

Contents

Acknowledgments

With my acknowledgment of assistance received comes a wish for blessings bestowed: Christmas gladness for all the year—with all that wish promises—to the community of believers who have participated in any way in the preparation of *Mary's Child*. My special gratitude goes to Anthony J. Cannon, Carla Cannon, Russell Orton, Cory Maxwell, Jana Erickson, Dan Hogan, Janna Nielsen, Harold Lundstrom, and helpful Church Historical Library researchers.

Prologue

Once upon a star-filled night, centuries before you ever received your first love-wrapped Christmas box, a babe was born in Bethlehem. That infant's cry resounded through heaven and earth. It was a signal for rejoicing. The birth itself was much like all other earth births except for one incredible difference: the babe was the Son of our Heavenly Father—*he was and is the Only Begotten Son of God in the flesh.* His mother was Mary, a virgin and a pure vessel chosen to be the mother of the Son of God. She named her miracle baby Jesus. He became known as the Christ.

Ever since, the whole season surrounding that sacred time has blossomed, becoming known as Christmas. Though the Christian world celebrates the birth of Jesus Christ on December 25, there is much evidence that the Messiah's birth was actually a prophesied event of Passover—commemorating that sacred time in spring when an angel of the Lord *passed over* the firstborn of the faithful as a sign of divine intervention during a tyrannical, hellish slaughter of Hebrew infants. Later, in the meridian of time, Mary's firstborn son entered mortality to be greeted by angels from heaven singing the song of songs—a momentous announcement of glory, joy, peace, and glad tidings to adorn the world—whether the world would realize it or not.

It was spring, and all the world awakened to new life. The loveliest of flowers bloomed—flags by the Jordan River, cactus roses in the desert, and lilies in the valley. Vines flourished among ancient stone. The palms were lush green, burdened with fat dates. The flat-leaf fig trees and the gnarled sage-green olive trees hung heavy with fruit. And then there was that brilliant new star, bringing an almost mystic air of tranquility with its miraculous appearance. It is said that contentment so laced the hour in which Jesus was born that even the animals were subdued, lowing and calling to each other gently.

Whatever the reckoning of the calendar—December 25 or April 6—and whatever the tradition of your personal seasonal celebration, life for all became more abundant and significant because of the birth of *that* baby! Indeed, we declare without hesitation that life itself, even all life prefiguring the Messiah's awaited coming, was enabled by the birth of that baby.

Ironically, this singular event was prophesied in ancient times, studied and discussed by scores and scores through the centuries, and yet the occurrence was noted as marvelous by only a handful of Earth's population; they were among the most humble people—shepherds, a carpenter, an innkeeper, a widow in the temple, and old Simeon who, before he departed this life, waited for a witness of the Messiah. Later, a tiny band of wise men from the Orient brought exotic gifts as part of their homage.

Tradition says:

> They were looking for a king
> To set them free and lift them high
> Thou cam'st a little baby thing
> To make a mother cry!

When word got around of a new king of the Jews appearing on the earth, the birth of Mary's child triggered yet another mass slaughter of infants under the command of Herod, king of Judea. As gossip mounted and both truth and legend concerning the Messiah spread from street corner to housetop, Herod became jealous to the point of fear-driven rage. Surely such devilish abuse of innocent life through tyrannical force evidences that the battle waged in heaven long ago between the followers of Satan and the disciples of Christ has carried over to Earth.

Mind you, that new babe, born in the manger near a humble village skirting Jerusalem, was not just an ordinary boy. Mary's Child turned out to be more than any of the neighbors could have imagined! Not only did he rise above the community confines of local Nazareth, he also embodied the truth later recorded in 1 John 5:4 that "whatsoever is born of God overcometh the world." Sweet and humble Jesus, the boyhood joy of Mary and Joseph, became the very way to "all that the Father hath." Succeeding generations of all mankind will be full of hope if they will remember Jesus and follow after him.

We who make up those succeeding generations worship Mary's Child. We count on his compassion, and we marvel at his tender mercies. He is our master and our link with Heavenly Father. He was born to bring to pass salvation for every human being ever born. There was no other way for life beyond the grave but through him.

Jesus was adored by precious Mary and her husband, Joseph. They patiently taught Jesus to develop spiritual strength, to work with his hands, to do carpentry, to manage survival skills for desert life, and to read from the sacred scrolls. From the first, Mary's Child was nurtured in the Hebrew traditions of their fathers. Family life in all its lovely realities helped the Child grow into the Man. Jesus grew and waxed strong before God. At a very early age he was filled with wisdom and knew all things. Mary's Child Jesus was prepared, lovingly trained to become the Messiah. He became the ideal for each of us to follow. That Holy Family—Mary the chosen mother, Joseph the foster father, Jesus the Son of God—is type and shadow for our own treasured units.

Just as humble Jesus was instructed in knowing how to fulfill his mortal assignment, so do we receive lessons in fulfilling ours. The brief parables and principles that Jesus taught while on earth, when applied by his followers, become magnificent truths for more perfect human relationships. They improve the quality of life and modify the natural human into a person of grace. For example, he clearly taught that those who exalt themselves will be humbled. It is a fact. It will happen. But those who are themselves humble ultimately will be exalted! Put in practical terms, when you sponsor a big dinner, it is unwise to always invite only rich neighbors or friends—they will simply invite you over for dinner someday to return the favor. Instead, try opening the feast only to the poor, the maimed, the lame, and the blind. Because such needful persons cannot hope to return the favor, you will be blessed and recompensed at the resurrection of the just. Instead of being rewarded with earthly accolades, the glory and credit will be noted in your ledger in heaven!

Jesus forgave the sinner and invited him back into the fold. He searched to recover the lost sheep, the missing coin, and the wandering person. He yearned to gather all under his protecting care, if only we would submit.

He was meek and unassertive, gently explaining the plan and purpose and principles of life. He spoke of the lofty place of the meek, the peacemaker, the humble in spirit, the pure in heart, the seeker after righteousness; of going the second mile and turning the other cheek. He taught us how to make heaven on earth, to live together in love.

He promised the mourners that he would not leave them comfortless but would visit them. That is a proven truth in my own life. He knows us by our names, by our spirits, by our works, and by our heartbreaks.

He taught people how to pray: to God the Heavenly Father of us all, but in the name of Jesus Christ who is our gate to Almighty God.

Jesus was the epitome of love and goodness, of unselfishness and obedience. He challenged us to become like him, for he knew this to be the only way of safety from sin on the only path to true happiness.

In premortal life, Mary's Child had prepared to live, teach, and serve on earth. There, under the command of God our Heavenly Father, Jesus was the Creator of the earth itself and all things in it. No wonder we weep as we sing, "How Great Thou Art!" Surely we are in awe surveying the first wildflowers of spring carpeting our alpine meadows in infinite variety!

He was earth-born in order to experience life in a body of flesh and blood (and so are we). Though his remembrance of life before this may have been dimmed (as our own is), Mary knew something of Christ's destiny. With her help Jesus sought the meaning of his own mission (as we must). He came to know who he was and to understand the will of God, his Heavenly Father. Though Jesus was a God too, he accepted the will of the Father in every instance and submitted in obedience, thus following the path required to atone for our sins. He died that all mankind might be saved. He became the necessary Redeemer in God's plan, suffering that we might not suffer if we would believe in him. Oh, it is wonderful that he should care so much for us!

After the suffering well-taken, appears the miracle. Our trials are opportunities to prove our faith. Then comes the flooding witness of Jesus.

On the third day after his crucifixion, Jesus rose from the garden tomb where he had been placed. He was from that moment a resurrected being. He appeared to his disciples, joining them for a meal of fish and honey. Later he appeared in ancient America to the descendants of the children of Israel who had fled the pending destruction of Jerusalem. He taught these Nephite people the principles of life eternal. Their records read, "[Jesus] did teach and minister unto the children of the multitude, . . . and he did loose their tongues, and they did speak unto their fathers great and marvelous things, even greater than he had revealed unto the people. . . . The multitude gathered themselves together, and they both saw and heard these children; yea, even babes did open their mouths and utter marvelous things." (3 Nephi 26:14–16.)

Jesus loved little children. *Mary's Child* is a gathering of stories—as seen through the eyes of the author—about historical mothers who nurtured and taught their babies to dedicate their time on earth to helping the Lord in his own incredible mission to bring to pass the immortality and eternal life of all mankind. A portion of the descriptions, commentary, and passages of dialogue in this book are not found in canonized texts, but are literary methods I have used to bring readers closer to the characters and achieve a more intimate mood. After all, it is from their lives that we glean valuable perspectives for our own.

For example, I was a mother in labor one Christmas Day

some years ago. Later, when I looked down at our daughter Holly cradled in my arms, I was aware of an exciting perspective about Mary in childbirth under the difficult circumstances of her day. I felt pangs of empathy and reverence for her. I had not fully appreciated her courage and stamina before. Furthermore, in preparing this book, I was blessed abundantly by my own miracle baby, Anthony Joseph, who was born under special circumstances according to his patriarchal blessing. He grew to be a man of scholarship and faith, a master teacher of truth, with the insight that I yearned for in a presentation such as this.

I had prayed my son Anthony (Tony, we called him) into being, claiming fulfillment of a promise in my own patriarchal blessing. He was born and lived and brought us incredible joy. When tragedy struck him as a young father, I tearfully felt the Lord's will. In prayer, I literally offered him back to Heavenly Father. As the day ended, April 6, 1997, Tony struggled briefly for the breath of life, then departed in that lovely season of Christ's birth, death, and resurrection, and the anniversary of the organization of his church in these latter days.

Jesus Christ lives still, communicating with mortals though based now in the world of spirits. It is not his birth alone that we celebrate at Christmas—it is his very life and his manner of living it. When considered thoughtfully, the hope that we can indeed follow his teachings, his life, his path changes our emotions and our desires, and prompts appropriate action at this glorious season.

Remembrance of Christ, like candles on the mantle, burns brighter at Christmas. Our joy is at its peak.

So again, we tell the story surrounding Mary's Child. Remarkable, insightful stories of his followers are also unfolded in this book, increasing our understanding that great men and women have been raised up in their day to serve the Lord Jesus, to do his will, and to be examples to each generation. The more of us who are increasingly like Mary's Child, Jesus Christ, and his disciples, the sweeter the miracle of Christmas.

May this book be joyous reading for you at Christmas and always—confirming your own experiences with Christ, strengthening your witness of him as our Savior, and reemphasizing the power that you have to help prepare others to make a magnificent difference in life as they serve the Lord.

Mary's Child

I n all the history of the world, never has a child risen to become greater than Mary's Child. Because of him, every mother who rears her children unto the Lord earns a place in the loving, holy heart of God.

Near the end of the first two thousand years of this earth's mortal history, an older woman known as Anne and her husband, Joachim, went before Heavenly Father in fervent prayer. At their advanced age, they were yet childless. Though the words of their plea were not recorded, according to tradition, an angel of the Lord appeared to Anne and declared: "The Lord has looked upon thy tears; thou shalt conceive and give birth, and the fruit of thy womb shall be blessed by all the world." A time later, Anne bore a lovely daughter, a child whom Joachim gave the name of Miriam, or Mary as she has been called in records ever since.

Traditionally known simply as the Virgin Mary's mother, the woman to whom this sweet child came is also called St. Anne. In parts of the Christian world, particularly in Brittany and Quebec, she is honored on July 26 with a feast day. St. Anne has been the subject of great paintings, one of the most famous being Leonardo da Vinci's work of the two famous mothers, *Virgin and Child with St. Anne*. The experiences and relationships of this grandmother of the Savior are reminiscent of other mothers whose lives in childbearing and rearing were marked by divine intervention and holy miracles, such as Sarah, Hannah, Elisabeth, Eunice, and Lois. (While not recorded in canonized scripture, information about St. Anne can be found in the Protoevangelion, or Apocryphal Gospel of James.)

The Bible picks up the story in the New Testament, where we learn of the unique mission that came to Mary. Mary was a beautiful young Hebrew woman who lived in Nazareth near Galilee. She was a virgin engaged to marry sensitive, lovable Joseph, who was of the house of David. Mary and Joseph were of the same heart and hope. We know from the way they conducted their lives that each had been carefully reared to be a true believer in the God of Abraham, Isaac, and Jacob.

God the Father sent his servant Gabriel to visit young Mary. I envision it was in the middle of a starlit night that Mary was awakened to receive a message that changed the world, let alone her own life! This singular event has become known throughout

Christianity as the Annunciation, because Gabriel "announced" to this innocent young woman her assigned, sacred role. Mary was to become the mortal mother of the Son of God, who was soon to come to the earth. According to the Bible's brief details, the astounding exchange between Mary and the angel Gabriel went something like this:

"Hail, thou that art highly favoured, the Lord is with thee." What comfort! God approved of her and was with her! But there was more. "Blessed art thou among women. . . . Fear not, Mary: for thou hast found favour with God," said Gabriel, who then proclaimed that she would conceive Jesus, "the Son of the Highest."

"How shall this be?" Mary asked the angel, startled at what he had said.

"The Holy Ghost shall come upon thee, and the power of the Highest shall overshadow thee: therefore also that holy thing which shall be born of thee shall be called the Son of God," explained the angel. "With God nothing shall be impossible."

Mary was stunned, yet within her soul beat a rhythm of faith and a warmth spread over her. She answered the angel saying, "Behold the handmaid of the Lord; be it unto me according to thy word." (See Luke 1:28–38.)

Reading between the lines one senses the sweetness, wonder, and faith of Mary. She had just been visited by an angel, who told her that she would bear the Son of the Almighty God! In humility she submitted her will, her life, to Deity's plan. Perhaps her Divine Son is not the only one in that sacred family from whom we have much to learn about obedience.

Afterward, Mary hastened to the house of her cousin Elisabeth to confess her miracle. In doing so, she praised God in a melodious, rapturous psalm, acknowledging that "he that is mighty hath done to me great things; and holy is his name" (Luke 1:49).

The coming baby would be hers—but not hers, after all. She was a vessel for conveying the Son of God to mortality. Yet because of this very circumstance of his human life and his unique eternal mission, Jesus would be more dear to her heart. Mary kept all these things and pondered them in her heart until that silent night when Jesus was born and she wrapped him in swaddling clothes and lay him in a manger. God had taught Mary about her baby before Jesus was born. She knew who he was and that, indeed, nothing with God or the Son of God was impossible. Yet when the future unfolded, each event and miracle and teaching that Jesus presented must have been a surprise to her. While Jesus grew, Mary matured in her own human way, as mothers must. She became a type and shadow for other mothers in every way. The whisperings of fulfillment are in each motherly heart as she provides a mortal tabernacle for a spirit child of God, but only through that child's keeping close to God can his or her true worth be realized.

Mary's son was trained in their home in Nazareth. Jesus was also inwardly prepared. Spiritually, he waxed strong with the necessary elements that would later be in readiness for higher and more divine contact.

When Jesus was grown, Mary became one of her son's first

converts and disciples. She was the catalyst for one of her son's first public miracles, which took place at a large wedding at Cana. The Apostles were there, too. It was here that Mary's faith was revealed along with the power of her divine Son. They were guests at a wedding; when the wine ran out prematurely, Mary described to Jesus the dilemma of their hosts: "They have no wine," she exclaimed. Mary did not tell Jesus what to do, she merely pointed out the problem. She confidently told the household servants, "Whatsoever he saith unto you, do it." Such instruction—strictly obeyed—can bring about miracles in our lives, as it did at this wedding feast. Jesus told the servants to fill the pots with water and serve it. However, rather than complaining at being served common water, distinguished wedding guests praised the hosts for their quality of wine. The disciples of Jesus knew the miracle, and believed in him. (See John 2:1–10.)

Not everyone listened to Jesus or honored his mother.

Approximately three years later, at the time of the outrageous insults and physical abuse on Jesus the Messiah—and the horrible details of the crucifixion itself—it was the Passover, just as it had been at his birth thirty-three years before. Mary stood by the cross of Jesus, bereft and struggling. As Jesus looked down from that tree of death, he noticed his mother and also the disciple which he loved. He uttered the tender words, which were the healing balm. "Woman, behold thy son!" Then to John the Beloved he said, "Behold thy mother!" The record emphasizes that from that hour John took Mary into his own home. (See John 19:26–27.)

Behind the prophets and special servants who have labored in behalf of Jesus' cause both before and after his earthly birth are lovely, caring mothers. Like Mary, they rear their babies into manhood equal to serving the Lord according to their own particular missions in life. Both the nurturing mother and the serving son take upon themselves the name of Christ and are at once blessed.

Elisabeth's Miracle Babe

I t is to Luke that we owe a debt of gratitude for much of the nostalgia that surrounds Christmas each year. The Gospel of Luke in the New Testament is a treasure in literature not only because of the sacred topic with which it begins but also because of the mood the author creates with the details he includes about the miracle of the birth.

Luke was a physician by profession and, we might surmise, a romantic by temperament, so his descriptions of people make them both real and important to us. We feel an affinity to them. Luke's twenty-four chapter account of Jesus is framed between angels announcing the births of John the Baptist and of Jesus Christ and angels announcing the resurrection of our Savior. Luke explained that even though others had written about what was "most surely believed," he felt justified in adding his testimony because he had a "perfect understanding of all things from the very first" (Luke 1:2–3). In other words, we can trust his version!

His flowing story begins with Elisabeth and her husband, Zacharias. (Even as the story of their child's conception and delivery sets the stage for that of Mary's miracle, so would their son's life prepare the way for her Holy Son's mission.) Elisabeth was surely one of the most choice of Heavenly Father's children. A daughter in the priestly line of Aaron, she was shown honor by being named after Aaron's wife, Elisheba, or Elisabeth. She was the daughter of a priest and the wife of a priest, Zacharias, who, though aged, was still a respected servant in the house of the Lord.

One evening many worshipers gathered at the temple watching for Zacharias to perform his priestly duty of lighting the incense. According to tradition, this was the innermost part of the worship of the day. The moment had come for Zacharias to spread the incense on the altar, as near as possible to the Holy of Holies. According to leading authorities on the period, priests and people would have reverently withdrawn from the neighborhood of the altar and prostrated themselves before the Lord, offering unspoken worship that likely included recognition of past deliverance, longing for mercies promised in the future, and entreaty for present blessings and peace. As Zacharias put a light to the incense, deep silence would have fallen upon the scene as the cloud of fragrance rose, symbolically carrying their prayers to heaven. Zacharias himself would then have bowed down in worship—except for a marvelous occurrence!

Suddenly this goodly old priest was startled by the appearance of "an angel of the Lord standing on the right side of the altar of incense" (Luke 1:11). Only Zacharias saw the angel! Only he heard the angel deliver a message from God that contained three astonishing promises:

1. His prayers had been heard—Elisabeth was to bear him a child, though she was an old woman past the years of childbearing.
2. Elisabeth's baby was to be a son and they were to name him John.
3. Because of his disbelief, Zacharias would be struck dumb until the day the baby was born.

When the angel had disappeared, the people waiting at the temple could tell that something unusual had happened to Zacharias, for when he recovered his wits, he gestured that he could not talk! Naturally, there was a great deal of conversation and supposition among the people. Perhaps because they perceived that Zacharias had seen a vision, they stepped back to leave a channel for him to pass through as he hastened home to Elisabeth.

Elisabeth and Zacharias lived in the hill country of Judea about four miles from the great temple in Jerusalem. It's not difficult for me to imagine what her life and home environment would have been like at the time of this great miracle. In the later years of her life, Elisabeth was worn from the work of caring for the ephod and the vestments Zacharias wore in the temple, pruning their grapevines, going to market, working the olive press, and shelling almonds. Yet happily she cooked savory meat with barley for the wholesome nourishment of her faithful, aging companion. Their home was a haven of warmth, love, and order. Though there never had been any children, Elisabeth was a gracious homemaker. Many good people of all ages gathered in their comfortable rooms to partake of the wisdom and hospitality of their old friends.

When Zacharias arrived home that evening, he must have embraced Elisabeth as usual, but then held her a moment or two longer. She wondered why and so asked. Alas, the poor man could not speak even to her. Amazing! What had happened? Through gestures and a writing tablet, Zacharias conveyed the message he had received from God. He also had to admit to her that he had doubted the angel's prophecy—that was why he had been struck dumb. How could these two old people become parents?

But faithful Elisabeth did not doubt. I imagine her response to be, "God's will be done!"

When she did conceive, she thrilled that the "reproach" of God had been taken from her. How marvelous a blessing! What an extraordinary situation this was. How could it be explained to anyone? If she circulated about, what might she say or do that would jeopardize this privilege? After all, Zacharias had been struck dumb as a sign! So Elisabeth hid herself away for five months, and the two of them grew spiritually in their retreat from the world to ponder the power of God in their affairs.

In the sixth month Elisabeth's cousin Mary came to visit her with news of yet another miracle! At Mary's first greeting to Elisabeth, the babe "leaped in [her] womb for joy," and Elisabeth was filled with the Holy Ghost. She knew that what Mary had to tell her was true, and she was thrilled that an angel had told Mary about Elisabeth's baby! Now they could marvel and console each other.

"Blessed art thou among women, and blessed is the fruit of thy womb," said Elisabeth.

Mary replied, "My soul doth magnify the Lord, and my spirit hath rejoiced in God my Saviour. . . . For he that is mighty hath done to me great things; and holy is his name." Her moving psalm of praise was filled with special insight.

Mary stayed three months with her cousin Elisabeth, during which time these two faithful women no doubt were lifted by intimate conversations as they humbly regarded the full meaning of the miracles in their respective lives. Then Mary returned to Nazareth. (See Luke 1:41–56.)

Just after Elisabeth's baby was born, their cousins, friends, neighbors, and people who worshiped at the temple came to the home to rejoice with them in this astounding occurrence. A beautiful infant of their very own proved that with God nothing is impossible! Surely there must be a special name for such a child, restless already in his olive wood crib. Elisabeth quietly said, "John." In surprise, the visitors questioned Elisabeth about choosing John instead of naming him after his father Zacharias. Further, they said, "There is none of thy kindred that is called by this name."

The relatives reacted strongly against naming this baby John. Of course, they hadn't heard the angel's instructions to Zacharias, who took a writing tablet and wrote, "His name is John."

Suddenly, before all those gathered, another miracle took place. The tongue of the faithful old temple worker was loosed, just as the angel had predicted. What a wonderful moment for Elisabeth—her miracle son was born, whom she could love and prepare for his ordained mission on earth. And Zacharias had been blessed with the return of his speech.

According to tradition among the Israelites, Zacharias conducted the circumcision of his son after eight days had passed. In a strong voice he pronounced upon him the name the angel had said God wanted for this special baby. Then, being filled with the Holy Ghost, Zacharias gave the baby John a father's blessing. In later records this blessing has been called a Benedictus, in which Zacharias prophesied that John would "be called the prophet of the Highest" because he would "go before the face of the Lord to prepare his ways; to give knowledge of salvation unto his people by the remission of their sins, through the tender mercy of our God." Elisabeth's baby was promised that he would give light where there was darkness and in the shadow of death he would guide others into the way of peace. John was to remember God's holy covenant with Abraham and help to fulfill it. (See Luke 1:58–80.)

Just as Zacharias had prophesied, and as Elisabeth had lovingly trained up her child, the baby grew up in holiness, righteousness, and strength before the Lord. Latter-day scripture reveals that in his youth, John "whom God raised up [was] filled with the Holy Ghost from his mother's womb," was baptized and ordained to do the work of a prophet. (See D&C 84:27–28.) He became known as John the Baptist because he spent his days living in the wilderness, baptizing, moving about without fear from enemies (as he had been promised by his father) to prepare a people to receive Jesus when he came to earth.

John became the ultimate example of what an Aaronic Priesthood bearer can and should be, for he held the keys of the preparatory gospel, which includes those principles needed to prepare people to come to Christ through baptism. Similarly, he personified the commitment and zeal evident in today's LDS missionary program, which anticipates and helps to prepare the world for the Second Coming of Christ.

Then, one holy, memorable day, John baptized Jesus. Because John was by now a holy servant and spiritually mature, he recognized the dove as a sign of the presence of the Holy Ghost, and he was privileged to hear the voice of God the Father introducing his Beloved Son. As Jesus took up his own mission to bring to pass the immortality and eternal life of all men, the followers of John became the disciples of Jesus.

John's influence waned. Yet there was no jealousy in John,

and his continued success was sufficient to catch the negative interest of Herod. Herod had John the Baptist imprisoned. Then he commanded the beheading of John in response to the insistent pleadings of his wicked wife, Herodias.

John's mission was completed. It was unique in all history. His service spanned three dispensations: he was the last of the prophets under the Law of Moses. He was the first of the New Testament prophets, and he came back to earth to bring sacred priesthood keys to the Prophet of the dispensation of the fulness of times. On 15 May 1829, John the Baptist bestowed the Aaronic Priesthood on the Prophet Joseph Smith and Oliver Cowdery in the name of Jesus Christ, the Son of God and Mary's Child.

Hagar's Son

Early in the second millennium before the Savior of the world entered mortality, Abraham and his household traveled to Canaan, living in tents that could be folded quickly for a stealthy move away from enemies or water shortage. The herds and the herdsmen, the bearers and the carriers, the servants and handmaids, wives, and children—all followed Abraham, in both his faith and his travels. This was not the first time the Lord had directed Abraham to settle elsewhere. For Abraham, home was wherever he propped his pastoral staff as he hearkened to the words of the Lord.

The definition of *family* at the time was inclusive of many varied relationships, all of whom were dependent on their spiritual and temporal leader for survival in this harsh land. Today, families of Christian, Jewish, and Islamic descent all trace their roots back to Abraham.

Class distinction was clear in those days of helpers and hand-maids answering to their masters and to the wives of such venerable men. Keeping concubines and slaves was an accepted social practice.

One choice woman of a lower class was destined to become known and revered by numberless concourses of people from many walks of life since that day—an Egyptian handmaid to Abraham's wife, Sarah. Her poignant story has become indelibly written among both secular and religious histories originating in that part of the world. Her name was Hagar, and she was a brokenhearted serving girl who, like some of us, once ran away from her problems. Later she was driven away. Indeed, the name *Hagar* means "flight."

As their days in Canaan lengthened, Sarah was getting on in years, and she had never borne a baby. For a woman in her position, this was both highly disappointing and personally quite embarrassing and caused much distress for the aging wife of a prophet. She thought on the matter for some time and finally arrived at what seemed like a good idea. If her handmaid Hagar had a child with Abraham, then Sarah could rear the baby as her own!

One night Sarah coaxed Abraham with soft words: "The Lord hath restrained me from bearing: I pray thee, go in unto my maid; it may be that I may obtain children by her" (Genesis 16:2).

Abraham was surprised at such a suggestion. Though this was the custom in some households in the day, Abraham and Sarah had been bonded for many years. Nonetheless, he wanted Sarah to be happy. He wanted his helpmeet to be content. He loved her, but he also needed to carry forth his own responsibilities: he had the Lord's work to perform and his scattered flocks and herds to mind.

Finally, Abraham hearkened to the voice of Sarah, and in time, Hagar conceived.

But soon Sarah's heart likely became influenced by the jealous tensions any woman in her position would feel, and the biblical record speaks of Sarah's harsh words to her husband regarding Hagar's condition. It seems Abraham was in a no-win situation. He had followed the insistent wishes of Sarah, and now she complained that Hagar despised her and that Abraham had wronged her. (See Genesis 16:45.)

"Thy maid is in thy hand; do to her as it pleaseth thee," Abraham said, perhaps a bit saddened that Sarah's will might do injury to his unborn child.

Sarah, overcome with jealously, abused Hagar. She dealt so severely with her handmaid that, in spite of the fact that she was pregnant, Hagar took flight into the parched wilderness. She was not prepared for a journey—she just escaped when the opportunity presented itself.

Frightened and thirsty, Hagar cried out to God, "Let me not see the death of this child!"

God, who is no respecter of persons, hears with great attention the cries of the lowly, the imperfect, and those who lack the courage to face a demanding situation undaunted. This is so to

the present time. We have but to call out in need, to knock, to
beseech him in prayer. Hagar, the desperate handmaid and
unwed mother-to-be, turned to the Lord for help.

Eventually, Hagar came to a spring of water and stopped to
refresh herself. She was there found by an angel sent from God
who spoke to her compassionately: "Whence camest thou? and
whither wilt thou go?"

"I flee from the face of my mistress Sarai," bemoaned Hagar.
She was undoubtedly humble and hopeful because God had sent
an angel to get her out of this dangerous predicament.

The angel instructed Hagar to return to her nomadic home,
submit to her mistress, and put herself in the care of the patriarch Abraham. In addition, Hagar learned that her baby would
be a boy who was known to God because of his part in the whole
plan for mankind: "Thou . . . shalt call his name Ishmael;
because the Lord hath heard thy affliction." *Ishmael* means "God
has heard."

There was more: Hagar was promised that her posterity
would become so great that they could not be numbered! Her
son, Ishmael, would be a man of the wilderness, dwelling in the
presence of all his brethren—a family man setting a pattern that
would last through the many generations. And so it has been to
this day.

Hagar praised the Lord for responding to her need by sending
an angel. Then, committed to patience and endurance for the
greater good of God's will over personal conflict, Hagar went back
to endure Sarah. When she was delivered of Abraham's son, they

called his name Ishmael. Abraham loved Ishmael and taught him the ways of desert life and of God. (See Genesis 16:6–16.)

Then, according to the timetable and will of God, Isaac was born to Sarah. The covenant between God and Abraham was completed. Hagar and Ishmael were sent away to establish their own lives in freedom. Ishmael's sons multiplied their race and spread north and west through Arabia. Their language, with few exceptions, was adopted in all the land. Down through the millennia since then, these people have looked through Ishmael to Abraham as their spiritual father.

Ishmael's early posterity is recorded in Genesis 25:12–19. They are listed in a place of honor among the generations of patriarchs and the twelve sons of Israel. Including Ishmael's first-born son, Nebajoth, the twelve princes in the family were Kedar, Adbeel, Mibsam, Mishma, Dumah, Massa, Hadar, Tema, Jetur, Naphish, and Kedmah. When Ishmael died, he was 137 years old. Thus, as promised, Abraham became the father of many nations, not just of Israel.

Because Hagar not only endured but also humbly heeded God's instructions as delivered by the angel, the promise given her was fulfilled. Through her son Ishmael, God's covenant with Abraham was also fulfilled as he became progenitor of number-less people in a multitude of nations. Scripture records, and Latter-day Saints firmly believe, God's words that one day every knee shall bow in every nation and recognize that Jesus Christ is the Father's Only Begotten in the flesh and that Mary's Christ is the Savior of all.

Rebekah's Twins

Ten camels loaded with gifts and goods followed the weary traveler from Canaan to Nahor. Though Eliezer was master of all the property of Abraham, the man was humble and worried about his errand. He was to choose a wife for the brilliant, charming Isaac. Abraham—and apparently God himself—doted on this young prince born so late in Abraham's life.

The camel train had reached a well of water on the outskirts of Nahor. This had been a tiresome journey that he did not want to go through again. He wanted no mistakes in finding the right woman for Isaac, so the conscientious servant of Abraham had a plan. Using his long stick to tap each beast of burden above its heavy-lidded eyes, Eliezer made his camels to kneel down beneath the cool shade trees of the oasis.

Then he himself knelt down and prayed, not only for his own success in this vital business but also to know the Lord's will concerning good Abraham's desires for his son. God's purposes must be met.

"O Lord God of my master Abraham, I pray thee, send me good speed this day, and shew kindness unto my master Abraham," Eliezer prayed. Then he specifically asked for the woman God had appointed for Isaac. Perhaps feeling insecure and even overwhelmed at such an assignment, the servant suggested a sign that might indicate if he chose correctly.

"Let it come to pass," the servant pleaded with the Lord, "that the damsel to whom I shall say, Let down thy pitcher, I pray thee, that I may drink: and she shall say, Drink, and I will give thy camels drink: also, let the same be she that thou hast appointed for thy servant Isaac; and thereby shall I know that thou has shewed kindness unto my master."

It was evening, and the women of the city usually walked leisurely to the well to draw water for the next day's needs. It was a gathering place. Events transpired exactly as the servant had prayed, except that he had not requested in his prayer that the Lord's chosen need be a woman of great beauty. But Rebekah was lovely and appealing. With the watering and drinking done, it was arranged—over two bracelets and an earring of heavy gold—that Eliezer's party could take lodging with the girl's family, who, it turned out, were relatives of Abraham and Isaac. Rebekah ran ahead to alert those at her home. (See Genesis 24:1–28.)

In these early times, mothers played a significant role in the development of their sons until they were about twelve years old. They were in charge of their education in all things, including spiritual training and character development—instilling attitudes of diligence, faithfulness, obedience, exactness, tender love, and mercy. Sarah had done well with her miracle baby, Isaac.

Planned marriages were a significant part of the mores early in the dispensation of the patriarchs. The chosen bloodline and the priesthood covenants made with the true God had to be preserved and protected by God's servants, each in his own time. Therefore, when it was Isaac's time to be married, his well-blessed, centenarian father took a deep interest in the matter, requiring Isaac to swear he would not to marry outside their realm or belief system. Even though Abraham and his families lived among the Canaanites, one of their local women would not do. So, when Isaac was forty years old, Abraham assigned Eliezer, who had long been a well-trusted steward over all the possessions of the great patriarch, to find a wife from among their relatives at Nahor.

For all that followed, there were two important factors that helped to meet God's eternal purposes. One was the character of Eliezer, the steward who was given the heavy responsibility of finding the right bride for Isaac. The second was the quality of the bride herself—she who would become the mother of Isaac's promised posterity—to help preserve God's covenants with Abraham. The importance of this can be perceived when we remember that such promises reach even into our own specific patriarchal blessings today! Rebekah was a woman through whom the Lord could work a significant and far-reaching phase of his plans for mankind.

The camel train of Abraham's servant reached Rebekah's hospitable family. Precious water was used to wash the feet of the steward and the men who traveled with the camels. They were fed and made comfortable. Then the timing was right for Eliezer to explain the purpose of his trip. He confessed to his prayer to Abraham's God regarding this choice. He exclaimed and praised Abraham's God for the immediate and exact answer for his prayer at the well! Rebekah's family agreed that it was not for them to go against God's purposes. "Rebekah is before thee, take her," they said. "Let her be thy master's son's wife, as the Lord hath spoken."

Abraham's servant fell to his knees and worshiped God in thanksgiving. Then they called Rebekah in to ask her if she would be willing to go with the servant back to Abraham and his son Isaac. She saw the pile of silver, gold, jewels, the exquisite raiment for her and the gifts for her family. She must have sensed the goodness of the steward, Eliezer, who had watched Isaac grow into manhood. She knew now that Isaac was of the right heritage for her to wed. She was a virgin and no more pleasant future awaited her. "I will go," Rebekah smiled. She agreed to go right away, as well, and not stay longer at home, not even for just ten more days, as her family had begged.

To this day, a marriage among the followers of the Lord is often accompanied by a family prayer circle with a father's blessing given upon the head of the bride. Rebekah received such a blessing from her father, Bethuel, and her brother Laban, who put their hands on her, telling her among other things, "Thou art our sister, be thou the mother of thousands of millions, and let thy seed possess the gate of those which hate them." A most significant promise, when viewed from this day thousands of years later, with the Holocaust still vivid in recent history.

After the blessing, Rebekah arose and left. She would be taken to Isaac, who had meditated and prayed about this venture. The camel train bearing Rebekah, her servants, and her most precious belongings wended a winding way to cross the Euphrates River, passed over the desert of sand near Damascus, and moved slowly beyond the highlands of Lebanon to the green beauty about the Sea of Galilee. From there they went to Beer Lahai-roi, the place of Hagar's well. Isaac saw them coming and hurried toward this important camel train, bearing a queenly Rebekah in robes of fine fabric. She quickly covered her face with her veil, as was the custom, and alighted from the camel to meet this chosen man who came quickly toward her. For such a woman as this had Isaac's life been spared by the appearance of an angel precisely at the moment Abraham had prepared to use the boy Isaac as a sacrifice at the altar of God. (See Genesis 24:32–67.)

Isaac took Rebekah into the tent that had belonged to his dear departed mother, Sarah. He loved Rebekah and was comforted by her.

And Rebekah conceived—twins!

Now we see the quality of motherhood that Rebekah would practice. The pregnancy was difficult and disconcerting. There seemed to be an unusual struggle within Rebekah's womb—a contention between the twins even before they were born! Rebekah prayed to the Lord for guidance and understanding. God made it known to Rebekah that two nations, two manner of people, were to be born to her. "The elder shall serve the younger," prophesied the Lord. Rebekah held this incredible information in her heart until the Lord's appointed time. (See Genesis 25:22–23.)

A spiritually oriented woman, the beautiful Rebekah was willing to be prompted by God in the care and management of her children. Even when she took action that seemed to go against tradition, she strictly obeyed her God, an example for mothers in every generation to follow in rearing their own babies.

The twins were named Esau and Jacob. As they grew, Esau was hairy and a cunning hunter, a man of secular focus who already had married two women of the Hittites, who worshiped different gods. Jacob was a refined man and a tent dweller, a man who worshiped at the altar of Jehovah, the true and living God. From the first, the boys themselves had marked their own ways. A casual verbal exchange made when they were young men later became a serious vow.

"Feed me, I pray thee, with some of that red pottage; for I am faint," said Esau.

"Sell me this day thy birthright," said Jacob.

So Esau sold his rights as the firstborn to his younger brother Jacob simply for a feast of soup or pottage of lentils. That is all the importance that Esau gave to his heritage! (See Genesis 25:29–34.)

Rebekah must have noted these things in Esau and was certain that she would be doing no harm to him if she guided Jacob instead of her firstborn into receiving the passing of the birthright from Isaac. Also, because God had spoken to her about the future responsibilities of Jacob, Rebekah was an especially loving and attentive mother to Jacob, all along the way. Responsibly, she imparted the love and security that strengthens self-esteem and comprehension of calling. Wittingly, she taught him the importance of applying religious beliefs to life. She helped him understand the wisdom of regarding family relationships from the perspective of the patriarch. She trained up her child in the way he should go.

Jacob obeyed his mother when she advised him to cover himself with the silken fur from the kidskin of goats and to put on the colorful robes of the first son, which she had woven in preparation for this very day. Then, while Esau was hunting, Rebekah made savory meat that she served the aged and blind Isaac. Jacob presented himself before his father, who felt the hairy skin, assumed the man before him was Esau, and pronounced the blessing of the birthright upon this son. When Esau did come to his father, Isaac pronounced on him a blessing of the "fatness of the earth, and of the dew of heaven from above," but also told him that Esau would live by his sword and serve his brother through the generations, until that day when he would get his dominion. (See Genesis 27:1–40.)

So Esau married one of Ishmael's daughters, a foretelling act of the two races in contention that exists to this day. Jacob, meanwhile, kept the faith. He took a camel train and went back to Laban, his mother's brother, for whom he worked seven years for Rachel but was given Leah, because of the tradition that the oldest girl must marry first. Then he received his beloved Rachel as his wife. Leah, Rachel, and their handmaids became the mothers of the twelve sons who bonded into their own families, language, and land. They became known as the twelve tribes, and Jacob was known as Israel.

Rebekah's son Israel kept the birthright and the covenant of God, thus preparing his people for the day when prophecy would be fulfilled regarding the birth of Mary's Child, the Savior and Redeemer of mankind.

Rachel's Joseph

Rachel's story is one of true love and heart-break, of struggle and astounding success, for she was the mother of Joseph. Joseph was sold into Egypt and rose to be second in command to Pharaoh and the noblest of men in two world cultures. To their loss, many people skip over the details of this Old Testament family's history, not recognizing that its intriguing elements make for a marvelous page-turning true story as love, honorably sought after, is thwarted through deceit and intrigue, and God's purposes are threatened by the adversary's influence while being supported by the courage of the faithful. Significantly, this Joseph was also the ancient ancestor after whom Joseph Smith, the Prophet of the Restoration, would be called, thus fulfilling a nearly four-thousand-year-old prophecy. (See 2 Nephi 3:14–15.)

Included in this spectrum of human interaction are personal frustration, falsehoods, miracles, temptations of power and greed, famine, life-threatening incidents, sibling rivalry, family squabbles, and sweet healing. With significant and sentimental similarities, relatives through many generations have walked the same path Jacob traveled—back and forth between Palestine and Egypt.

The players in the drama include the patriarch and common father to the twelve tribes of Israel, Jacob, as well as the powerful pharaoh of Egypt. Though much could be written about the male figures who influenced Joseph's life—including those who sold him into bondage—we will focus on Rachel and her son, two extraordinary disciples of Mary's Babe Jesus.

The incredible story begins with Jacob, a lonely traveler making his way on the ancestral path between Canaan and Haran. This Jacob was a son of Isaac, who was a son of Abraham. Rebekah was his beloved mother, and Esau his estranged twin. Jacob was sent from his father's house with a blessing and a charge that he should not marry a wife from among the Canaanites; instead, he must go to his mother's family to find a proper partner.

Jacob had been given the birthright, and he lived with abiding faith. While sleeping one night on his journey from Canaan to Padan-aram, Jacob saw in vision angels ascending a ladder into heaven. The Lord God was standing above it, uttering a magnificent blessing on Jacob. A true believer, Jacob made an impressive vow that pointedly reveals to us that God's covenants and commandments apply in all generations. Jacob promised, "Of all that thou shalt give me I will surely give the tenth unto thee." And Jacob became a full-tithe payer. As Jacob continued his journey, God blessed him beyond his wildest dreams. He met Rachel, one of the most beautiful women mentioned in the Bible, in a lyrical, pastoral setting. It was late spring, the earth was at its most breathtaking, the morning air was cool, and the fragrance of saffron lifted from the meadow. Jacob viewed the valley of his ancestors. Grazing sheep were being gathered to the ancient watering hole. Shepherds rolled away the protective stone from the well so that the animals could lap their fill.

Suddenly, a striking young woman appeared, a bright-eyed beauty gracefully robed in the colorful fashion of her people. She had been watching over her father's flock and therefore carried the traditional curved staff of a shepherd.

When Jacob asked the other shepherds at the well who she was, they introduced him to Rachel, daughter of Laban.

Jacob's heart stirred at such good fortune. Rachel was his cousin! She was from the right family! The object of his journey was to find a proper wife—could Rachel possibly become his own?

Later, Jacob confessed that for him it was love at first sight. There in the field of grasses, herbs, blossoms, and gentle lambs beside the ancient well, Jacob boldly kissed Rachel. Perhaps it was intended as a traditional kiss between cousins at first, but clearly the mutual attraction between the two young people was immediate. Rachel, blushing and smiling, quickly led the way to her father's home. Jacob took her hand and followed with weak knees.

As fate would have it, years before at this same well, Laban's sister (Jacob's mother Rebekah) had drawn water for Grandfather Abraham's faithful servant. That servant had been sent to find a wife for Abraham's son Isaac. God had readied Rebekah. Now, hopefully, another family link was to be established.

The way of love is rarely smooth. Jacob begged Laban for permission to marry Rachel, but Laban wanted him to marry Leah, the older sister. Laban's terms were hard—Jacob was to abide with his Uncle Laban, working seven years in his field. The promise of Rachel was exciting at any price, so Jacob agreed.

"I will serve thee seven years for Rachel thy younger daughter," said Jacob.

Meanwhile, Laban plotted to deceive the bridegroom. After seven long years, the appointed time arrived. The Bible speaks of Jacob's devotion during that time in one of the most romantic descriptions in all the world's literature: "And Jacob served seven years for Rachel; and they seemed unto him but a few days, for the love he had to her." It was now the wedding night, and Jacob's anticipation was keen. Secretly Laban substituted in the marriage bed the sullen Leah for the glowing, lovable Rachel of Jacob's heart. In the morning Jacob realized what had taken place; overwhelmed by anger and frustration, he confronted Laban: "Did I not serve with thee for Rachel? wherefore then hast thou beguiled me?"

Laban's callous reply stunned Jacob: "It must not be so done in our country, to give the younger before the firstborn. Fulfill her [Leah]!"

Laban growled that if Jacob really wanted Rachel, he could work another seven years. Jacob no doubt wondered why Laban had not explained before about his country's wedding rules regarding an unmarried older sister. But ever the man of integrity—and still deeply in love with Rachel—Jacob agreed to do his duty. At long last they were married. Some said the stars in Rachel's eyes rivaled the night sky!

In time, Leah gave Jacob several sons, while Rachel produced none; nonetheless, Jacob "loved also Rachel more than Leah" (Genesis 29:30). Inevitably sibling rivalry increased in that polygamous arrangement. Jealousy plagued both the plainer, older woman and her charming, younger sister. Finally, following an agonizing wait, Rachel gave birth to her first baby—Joseph, a child who would become the jewel of Egypt. Joseph was nurtured in an atmosphere of love. A refined woman of faith, Rachel carefully tutored Joseph in Godlike attributes and instilled within him the good and gracious principles to live by that would benefit a humble servant of the Lord. Jacob favored Joseph, and though he taught the lad the work of the fields, a favored child by a favorite wife is the stuff from which trouble is often brewed.

Life was not a calm sea for Jacob's family, and in addition Laban had been consistently unfair with Jacob. Enough was enough! Jacob felt the hand of God guiding him back to Isaac and Rebekah, his faithful parents. There was the matter of the birthright, too. So, while Laban was away shearing the sheep, Jacob took all of his family—with the herds that he felt were rightly his own—and secretly moved them from Haran. They followed the same ancestral path back across the green meadows and desert sands to Canaan.

Among the covenant people of Abraham, the birthright was given to the son who was worthy before God, regardless of his order of birth in the family. Leah's sons were older, but Rachel's Joseph was given the birthright. The sun's golden rays were to shine on Joseph forever. With that honor went the signifying coat of many colors, which Rachel probably made.

Joseph grew in resourcefulness, spiritual insight, and compassion. Joseph also grew to be hated by his brothers. The jealous older half-brothers connived to get rid of the younger one. Joseph was taken on a hunting trip and sold as a slave in Egypt. With the blood of a slain lamb, the brothers stained the royal coat of many colors, taking it home to Jacob as proof of Joseph's death.

Jacob was bereft. Little did he know that Joseph's mission was already underway. Throughout history, God has worked, protecting and guiding his faithful children so that ultimately his eternal plan will be realized. Thus, Potiphar, an officer of Pharaoh, bought Joseph as a slave and installed him as a steward in his own home. He noticed that the Lord was always with Joseph, so much so that the young man prospered in all that he did. The Egyptian was blessed because of Joseph!

Ironically, despite the fact that the Lord obviously smiled

brightly on Joseph while he was in Potiphar's household, Joseph also received his most well-known temptation in that same household. In an incident with Potiphar's wife, Joseph became the singular example for all time of a person who would not fall to temptation, no matter what. Joseph was repeatedly harassed by Potiphar's wife, even exquisitely lured into a trap with a threat. But Joseph was valiant! The moral course of action in such a situation in any time frame is found in this biblical account: Joseph "left his garment in her hand, and fled, and got him out" (Genesis 39:12).

Joseph's experiences and contributions in the land of Pharaoh were of long-lasting importance. Four thousand years later, we would be wise to note the following truths:

• Joseph always remembered how his mother, Rachel, had prepared him for the exigencies of life and service to the God of Israel.

• Joseph rose to a high point of leadership in Egypt, second only to Pharaoh, gaining that position because of his hard work, honesty, and willingness to follow the Lord's directions.

• Joseph was given, by God, the spiritual gift of interpreting dreams. Pharaoh believed and gave Joseph the lead in preparing for the famine which he had prophesied.

• Joseph, clearly inspired, established a grain storage program for the welfare of Pharaoh's people during the crisis of famine. He later used this program to reunite himself with his family at a critical time, literally saving all their lives.

• Joseph became fluent in the Egyptian language. Thus,

years later, when the stepbrothers came to the land of Pharaoh to buy grain during the famine, Joseph was able to disguise himself before them for his own purposes.

• Joseph returned good for evil. Finally he was reunited with his beloved younger brother, Benjamin, whose mother also was Rachel. Significantly, Benjamin was a direct ancestor of the Apostle Paul, who spoke of this heritage publicly.

• Joseph sent supplies and *wagons* to carry his aged father and his entire entourage of 70 persons, plus their herds and belongings, all the way to the land of Pharaoh. They settled near Goshen in choice land authorized by Pharaoh himself!

• Joseph loved and honored his father. He made ready his own chariot and went up to meet Israel. He presented himself unto him, then "he fell on his [father's] neck, and wept on his neck a good while. . . . And Joseph brought in Jacob his father, and set him before Pharaoh: and Jacob blessed Pharaoh" (Genesis 46:29; 47:7).

• Jacob gave Joseph a father's blessing, which promised that Joseph would have the blessings of heaven and the deep that lieth under. Joseph was described as a "fruitful bough, even a fruitful bough by a well; whose branches run over the wall." He was promised that the blessings of his father and progenitors "unto the utmost bound of the everlasting hills " would be on the head of Joseph. (See Genesis 49:22–25.)

• Joseph married a woman named Asenath, who bore Ephraim and Manasseh. Father Israel blessed the two sons of Joseph, crossing his hands and once again giving the birthright to the younger son. It is through these two grandsons of Jacob and Rachel that many Latter-day Saints trace their sacred heritage.

• Joseph nurtured his father and all his family until Jacob was 147 years old. When the faithful patriarch died, Joseph "fell upon his father's face, and wept upon him and kissed him" (Genesis 50:1). As a special courtesy, Joseph commanded the physicians of Pharaoh to embalm Jacob's body.

• Joseph led a funeral parade of grand pomp and ceremony— all that Egypt could produce. The units included the elders and people from all the houses of Pharaoh, as well as Joseph's own, and those of all his brethren. Once again, there was a trek across the desert sands as they buried Jacob with his ancestors near Machpelah in the land of Canaan.

• Joseph's entire life had been to follow the duties of his birthright and to make a unique contribution to the holy mission of Jesus Christ. He died at 110 years of age. He too was embalmed, but he was placed in a coffin in Egypt, with the request that his bones be taken to Canaan. Following Joseph's death the Israelites increased and flourished until there came a Pharaoh "which knew not Joseph" or his increasing relatives. The stage was set for the children of Israel to be taken into captivity and for Moses to rise up and lead the Exodus.

What of Rachel, the mother of this man Joseph?

When Joseph and his father were reunited in Egypt, Joseph learned how deeply his father had always loved his mother. In a poignant sharing, Jacob explained Rachel's death in childbirth with Benjamin: "When I came from Padan, Rachel died by me in the land of Canaan in the way, when yet there was but a little way to come. . . . I buried her there in the way of Ephrath; the same is Bethlehem." (Genesis 48:7.)

Together these two great men wept remembering Rachel.

Rachel's burial place is still marked outside of Bethlehem. It is the oldest individual memorial to a woman included in the Bible. She is the first woman mentioned in the Bible to die of childbirth. Rachel, with Leah and their handmaids Bilhah and Zilpah, established the house of Israel through the seed of Jacob. Their twelve sons were designated as the Twelve Tribes of Israel.

Special recognition is given to Rachel by the members of the kingdom of God on earth today. Rachel brought forth and prepared Joseph. In about 600 B.C. a large group of his posterity left Jerusalem just before its destruction. This group followed the God-given Liahona and made their way to ancient America, where they established two great nations. The gospel of Jesus Christ was preserved on metal plates, and He was with them.

Jochebed's Baby

The bulrushes and flags swayed gently along the bank of the Nile River, where swamp moss crowded the slimy shore. This was a perfect place to hide a three-month-old baby. The Egyptians were cruelly and rapidly wiping out a whole generation of male infants among the God-fearing Hebrews held captive by the Egyptian Pharaoh. Her son of destiny must not be one of them. No longer could Jochebed keep her baby hidden at home. She must find a new way to hide him.

It's apparent that Jochebed's love for this son was deep—shaped not only by her natural maternal longings but also by her spiritual whisperings that implied so much. When Jochebed's baby was newly born, she realized in a way that mothers can that this son was a "goodly child." He was so well formed and beautiful to look upon. She had other children that she dearly loved, but this one—this one was meant for some special mission. Surely the boy would be used by the Lord for his purposes someday—if he lived so long! She was hopeful for his future, yet so fearful of his present danger. So much depended on her that she knew she must be wary, as well as wise, in protecting him. She yearned for a solution that would permit her to train him as the servant of the Lord he needed to become.

Now as she walked by the Nile she knew she had been led there. Jochebed gathered rushes and reeds and wove them into an ark just large enough to hold her baby. She sealed it with pitch, daubed it with thick slime, then she packed it with moss from the shoreline. When it was ready, Jochebed gently placed her baby on the moss. The boy's mother and sister carefully helped float the ark among the bulrushes. Then the sister hid herself to keep watch on the baby.

Soon the daughter of Pharaoh came to that very spot on the river to bathe, leaving her handmaids on the shore to secure her privacy. The sister's heart pounded: had God prepared such a rescue for this baby? Maybe. It was marvelously ironic that this child's savior might be someone from the enemy's household; yet, given the right circumstances, the boy's future could possibly mean help for all his people currently suffering as slaves to the powerful Pharaoh.

Then it happened! Pharaoh's daughter saw the floating ark among the thick vegetation at the water's edge and sent one of her maidens to fetch it. When the royal daughter looked inside, the infant cried, and she had compassion on him. "This is one of the Hebrews' children!" she exclaimed. (See Exodus 2:5–10.)

This touching scene must have been full of tenderness and love. "Little one, be at peace. Shhhh," Pharoah's daughter cooed to the crying infant. She was filled with empathy, eager to hold the infant and comfort him.

Jochebed's daughter, from her hiding place in the reeds, saw Pharaoh's daughter lift the crying infant out of the woven ark and hold him in her arms. All the handmaids had gathered around and were cooing and sighing in the way women will with an infant. So the baby's sister stood from her hiding place unnoticed and walked toward them to look upon the babe as if in curiosity.

"Shall I go and call to thee a nurse from among the Hebrew women?" the little girl asked. "That she may be a nurse for the child for thee" (Exodus 2:7). This was entirely an appropriate suggestion, because the Hebrews were enslaved by the Egyptians and often served as nursemaids.

"Go," commanded Pharaoh's daughter.

So the little girl hurried back to their home to get her own mother. And I imagine that this scene was even more joyous than that just witnessed. The two hugged each other in excitement. Then Jochebed offered one more prayer before she left her home and walked to the place by the river. Her heart was pounding wildly. Would she find her babe alive and well? Could she find peace in seeing her own infant in the arms of an Egyptian woman? Could she feel God's Spirit confirming that this was a *right* thing in ways she couldn't understand yet? Jochebed's mind raced, then settled in faith in God as she reached the place where she had left her chosen child not long before.

Jochebed bowed before Pharaoh's daughter, who continued to hold the baby as she addressed the Hebrew woman, not knowing that Jochebed was the baby's true mother. A quick conversation ensued.

"This baby needs a nursing mother for a time."

"That seems true enough," replied Jochebed, praying to still her ruffled soul.

"You can do this?"

Jochebed nodded.

"I will give you wages if you will nurse him until he has sufficiently grown."

The baby's sister gasped, calming herself at once so as not to reveal their relationship. The infant's mother had to swallow her tears of joy. God had heard her prayers. Her baby was not dead. There was time ahead—precious time—in which she could teach the baby the things God wanted him to know.

So Jochebed sang to her special baby, recited sayings and traditions of the Hebrews, and gave him more of herself than mother's milk. The child never forgot his real heritage, not even after Pharaoh's daughter, a foster mother of ways and means, gave the boy rare advantages. It was clear that she yearned after her adopted son. And Jochebed was grateful to God.

Pharaoh's daughter said, He shall be called Moses, "because I drew him out of the water" and I will raise him as my son. (See Exodus 3:10.) Indeed, *Moses* means "drawn." Pharoah's daughter gave him every advantage—position with appropriate attention, education, and all the training in skills to which a young Egyptian prince was entitled. Pharaoh's daughter was thrilled to have come by such a remarkable child for her own.

Moses grew and filled a life marked with great magnitude. In time, he was in a position to negotiate with his foster mother's father, who favored Moses. With the Lord's authority, Moses performed many miracles and signs in an attempt to satisfy Pharaoh and achieve the release of the Hebrews from their insufferable captivity under the Egyptians.

In humility, holiness, and effectiveness, Moses compassionately gathered together Heavenly Father's chosen Israelite children and led them through the Red Sea, through the wilderness, and to the promised land. He was the prophet of manna, the burning bush, and the Ten Commandments, which faithful people live by to this day, and he consecrated Aaron and his sons in the priesthood. He was a proper man of indomitable faith who talked with God "face to face" in Sinai and beyond, learning the beginning and the end of the plan and the purpose of all creation. Moses also wrote records included in the Bible and latter-day scriptures. Paul spoke of him: "By faith Moses, when he was come to years, refused to be called the son of Pharaoh's daughter; Choosing rather to suffer affliction with the people of God, than to enjoy the pleasures of sin for a season; Esteeming the reproach of Christ greater riches than the treasures in Egypt. . . . By faith he forsook Egypt, not fearing the wrath of the king: for he endured, as seeing him who is invisible." (Hebrews 11:24–27.)

Moses ordained Joshua by the laying on of hands as the Lord commanded him. Remarkably, miraculously, Moses did not taste of death. The Lord "took Moses unto himself." (See Alma 45:19; Deuteronomy 34:7.) He was 127 years old, but his eye was not dim nor his natural force abated when he was seen no more in Moab. The children of Israel wept and mourned for him for thirty days.

Moses was a translated being—since the Resurrection had not taken place yet—who returned to be seen at the time of the Transfiguration of Christ on the mount, and again to deliver keys of the priesthood to Joseph Smith and Oliver Cowdery in the Kirtland Temple. The ministry of Moses extended beyond the limits of his own mortal lifetime.

In a wiping away of time, Moses became linked with Mary's Baby. Jochebed, the mother of Moses, is honored because she prayed over him and unselfishly gave up her son rather than see him killed. She taught him well, and he is remembered in the scriptures for his meekness as well as his leadership, his dignity as well as his faithfulness to God.

Moses, the son of Jochebed and the foster son of Pharaoh's daughter, found favor as a special servant to the God of the Old Testament, he who became the Messiah in the New Testament, even Jesus, the Child of Mary, through a miracle in the meridian of time!

Hannah's Man Child

Hannah was a noble Jewish woman who lived almost twelve centuries before the Common Era marked by the birth of Jesus. She was descended from a significant priest and prophet named Levi, the son of Jacob and leader of one of the twelve tribes of Israel. Hannah's comfortable life was befitting a person of such noble station. Her husband, Elkenah, loved her, always giving her more than what the custom of the day required for a man to bestow on his wife. In addition, Elkenah was tender and sympathetic with her. What more could a woman ask?

Yet, Hannah had a problem. She had not given her husband an heir. Year after year her prayers for a child went unanswered. In her mind, this sadness in her life must have far outweighed the blessings, and as time passed, Hannah became increasingly distraught.

"The Lord has shut my womb," she would wail in an emotional outcry typical of the women in her day. It was the duty and the pride of a Jewish woman to be a mother, but Hannah had been denied this privilege. Elkenah, distressed over Hannah's shame and misery, remonstrated with her.

"Hannah," questioned Elkenah, "why weepest thou? . . . and why is thy heart grieved? Am I not better to thee than ten sons?" (1 Samuel 1:8.)

But Hannah would not be comforted. Bitter sorrow flooded her soul. One year, when the time came again for the family's annual pilgrimage to make a sacrifice to the Lord of Hosts in Shiloh, Hannah decided to carry forth a plan. She would prepare more than supplies for the journey—she would make *herself* ready, spiritually, through fasting and repentance, to kneel humbly at the altar of the Lord and plead for motherhood.

At the temple of Shiloh, Hannah poured out her heart, making a firm vow to God that if he would remember his handmaid in her affliction and give her a "man child," she would give him back as a gift. "I will give him unto the Lord all the days of his life," Hannah promised.

Nearby, the priest Eli watched Hannah in her anguish. Her lips moved, but he heard no sound so he accused her of being intoxicated. Hannah explained that she had been speaking out of the abundance of her complaint and grief. She was weak from fasting and praying for a child.

Eli answered, "Go in peace: and the God of Israel grant thee thy petition."

Elkenah and Hannah returned home to Ramah, and in time a baby boy was born to them. Hannah named him Samuel, which means "name of God." (See 1 Samuel 1:9–20.)

Hannah marveled at the perfect little infant, nuzzling him to her in joy. Hannah loved Samuel. All the while she nursed him, she whispered eternal truths into his ear, and confessed the goodness of God. She smoothed the hairs of his infant head and stroked across the shoulders of his small frame.

In Jewish tradition, a baby is the mother's sole domain until well past early childhood. Furthermore, Jewish boys were nursed much longer than girls, and in delight Hannah kept Samuel and did not go herself to the temple until he was weaned. Then, with generous stocks of food and supplies, Hannah presented Samuel at the temple of God and left him in the care of the priest Eli, in keeping with her vow of sacrifice.

"For this child I have prayed," said Hannah, "and the Lord hath given me my petition which I asked of him: Therefore also I have lent him to the Lord; as long as he liveth he shall be lent to the Lord" (1 Samuel 1:27–28).

There at Shiloh, the child ministered before the Lord, "girded with a linen ephod." Fifteen centuries before the birth of Christ, there was a religious tradition concerning fabric for temple service. It was in this regard that Hannah made a "little coat" for her son from colorful fabric. Exodus tells us that "all the women that were wise hearted did spin with their hands, and brought that which they had spun, both of blue, and of purple, and of scarlet, and of fine linen" (Exodus 35:25). Samuel's ephod was like that worn by bearers of the priesthood in the temple, shaped like a waistcoat and made of rich colors—blue, purple, scarlet—with onyx stones on each of the shoulder pieces. There was a girdle to go about the waist. These vestments symbolized their mission of priesthood service to carry the burdens of the people. Each year as the family went to sacrifice at Shiloh, Hannah took a new priestly outfit that she had lovingly made for Samuel to meet his growth in stature and his needs as a servant of God. And Samuel remembered what his mother had done for him.

While in the temple, Hannah gave this song of thanks and praise: "My heart rejoiceth in the Lord, mine horn is exalted in the Lord. . . . There is none holy as the Lord: for there is none beside thee: neither is there any rock like our God. . . . The Lord is a God of knowledge, and by him actions are weighed." (1 Samuel 2:1–3.)

As a child Samuel did not have a personal knowledge of the Lord, nor had the word of God been revealed fully to him. But one night a marvelous thing happened. Samuel was awakened from a deep sleep by someone calling his name. The boy was startled and ran to Eli, because he assumed it was he who had called. "Here am I," Samuel cried, "for thou calledst me." Eli denied having called the boy's name, so Samuel tumbled back into his bed. Then the same awakening happened a second time. Still, a third time, Samuel was called from sleep and heard the call and ran to Eli, who told Samuel that if he heard the call again, he would know that it was from the Lord. He was to answer the Lord and listen, later reporting to Eli all that was said.

After Samuel went back to bed, he was indeed awakened a fourth time. This time young Samuel replied, "Speak; for thy servant heareth."

Samuel's life was never the same again, for that night the Lord talked with him about many of the marvelous things in store for God's children on earth. And Samuel was called to help him! After that, the Spirit of the Lord was with Samuel always. The boy grew into a pure man and found favor with God and man. He was honored and respected by his people as a man whose prayers were heard by the Lord. (See 1 Samuel 3.)

For example, at one point the children of Israel were in terrible disarray because of the Philistines' constant assault on them. Samuel spoke firmly to all the Israelites that God was their only hope. "Prepare your hearts unto the Lord, and serve him only: and he will deliver you out of the hand of the Philistines. . . . and I will pray for you unto the Lord," Samuel promised. (1 Samuel 7:3–5.)

The people began to heed Samuel's words. They changed their lives and drew close to the Lord. They were overcome with joy because Samuel's prayers for them were heard by the Lord. The next time the Philistines came in mighty battle against Israel, that very day the Lord "thundered with a great thunder upon the Philistines" until they all were smitten before Israel!

Then came peace. All the people between Dan and Beersheba knew that Samuel was established as a mighty prophet.

The Lord continued to reveal himself—through his word—in Shiloh to Samuel.

Samuel was counselor and advisor attending the unstable Saul, until the king's sin and rebellion against the Lord forced Samuel from helping Saul further. Later, Samuel risked his own life because of Saul's anger when the Lord told Samuel to go to Bethlehem to the house of Jesse. "I have provided me a king among his sons," said the Lord.

Samuel said, "How can I go? If Saul hear it, he will kill me." Saul still wanted to be king!

But obedient Samuel did as the Lord commanded. He took a heifer to offer in sacrifice to the Lord, and he invited the house of Jesse to join him. Samuel looked upon each of Jesse's fine sons, sensing that any one of them could be a king. When Jesse asked if there were yet another son, young David was brought from the fields where he watched over the sheep, practiced with his sling-shot, and played his lute. Samuel took oil, and anointed David there before his father and his brothers. The Spirit of the Lord came upon David from that day forward. (See 1 Samuel 16.)

David, who slew Goliath, became a noble, beloved leader of the Israelites. Samuel was by David's side for many years of his reign.

The goodly prophet Samuel restored law and order in all the land and established regular religious worship in the land. He became a judge to all Israel, going from year to year in circuit to Bethel, Gilgal, and Mizpah—mediating, preaching, and judging in all those places. Then he returned to his house in Ramah, where he had built an altar unto the Lord.

Samuel, Hannah's baby boy, grew into a prophet of influence and humility. He had been given a good start because of Hannah's persistence and preparation to receive answers to her prayers, which resulted in her love and teaching of her "man child" whom she gave back to the Lord. Samuel, all the days of his life, was a beloved servant in the cause of Mary's Child, the Lord Jesus Christ.

Bathsheba's Infant

In King David's time, the houses in Jerusalem and the surrounding country were made of sandstone with versatile flat roofs to meet the needs of the family living there. There, in the open air on top of the house, the women could grind grains for unleavened bread, dry fruit, prepare food, cure meat, and hang up wet laundry and dyed woven goods to dry. In the cool evenings the roof was used for sleeping, for personal cleansing, and for water storage. Such houses can be seen to this day in both Egypt and the Holy Land.

Bathsheba lived in such a house. One evening she was bathing herself on the roof just when King David walked along his roof. He looked down upon her and desired this unusually beautiful, intelligent, and well-spoken neighbor. Any woman in that day was subject to the command of the king, so she was in no position to resist David's servants when they were sent to bring her back to him.

Bathsheba lay with David and conceived a child. Sinful plotting by the king to have the woman's husband killed in battle freed Bathsheba to marry David. Their first baby, conceived out of wedlock, died. After they were married, Solomon was born.

Great remorse and heavy penalties followed, providing a theme for the psalms of David, many of which are full of such anguished phrases as, "Create in me a clean heart, O God" (Psalm 51:10). There seems to have been no extenuating circumstance to justify what David had done. But we should consider Bathsheba's baby, born of her union with David, who became the great Solomon.

Setting aside the mortal tendency to judge others, we would do well to remember the ample evidence that God assigns the eternal spirit that gives life to a tiny baby conceived by mortals. Legal or illegal, authorized or unauthorized, unduly sweet or shamefully sinful, convenient or inconvenient, ready or not, given a certain set of circumstances, there is a newborn. In this case the infant was Bathsheba's baby, who received a spirit that was unlike any other, a spirit beloved of the Lord. And, oh, how Bathsheba loved her Solomon!

On this particular matter, little was recorded that still remains that we might sift through for a fine point of truth, but all that we really need to know is that King David and Bathsheba each gave of themselves the genetic heritage, the spiritual training, and the social and cultural constitution that had made them desirable people. Solomon's remarkable heritage from King David, son of Jesse, would become one day the lineage of Jesus Christ. Bathsheba is to be credited with recognizing a choice spirit in her son Solomon. This was not merely a loving mother's wishful thinking; rather, Bathsheba was clearly an inspired woman who responded to spiritual leaders, as later events prove. Her faith assured her that God had a wise purpose for Solomon. She would help bring this about. Also, ultimately, Bathsheba would be an ancestor to the Messiah.

When David was very old and in need of much ministering, Bathsheba learned that one of David's sons had made a feast with a great host of followers and was waiting for David to die so that he, Adonijah, could sit on the throne. The prophet Nathan counseled with Bathsheba about this serious turn of events, and she did exactly as he said. She went into David's chamber and used finesse and deference befitting his position as king.

"What wouldest thou?" the king asked Bathsheba.

"My Lord, thou swearest by the Lord thy God unto [me] thine handmaid, saying, Assuredly Solomon thy son shall reign after me." Then Bathsheba told David all that had transpired from the feasting to Adonijah's claiming the right to the throne. She said, "My lord, O king, the eyes of all Israel are upon thee, that thou shouldest tell them who shall sit on the throne of my lord the king after him. Otherwise it shall come to pass, when my lord the king shall sleep with his fathers, that I and my son Solomon shall be counted offenders."

As she finished her respectful obeisance, the prophet Nathan was announced; he entered and bowed before the king. He asked after the matter of King David's successor—Adonijah or Solomon.

"Bathsheba," called out David. She stood again before him, and he repeated his oath to name Solomon as his successor to the throne, affirming, "I will certainly this day."

"Let my lord king David live for ever," said Bathsheba bowing with her face to the floor, her silk and flaxen robes dusting the mosaic floor as she backed away from him. (See 1 Kings 1:11–31.)

That very day Solomon rode on David's mule to a high place, and Zadok the priest anointed Solomon with oil. According to David's wishes, a great trumpet sounded, and all the people said, "God save King Solomon."

Bathsheba's victory proved her position with the king. Bible scholars have pointed to this incident as the important mission of Bathsheba's life, because it brought Solomon to the throne. Solomon had responded to her tutoring and nurturing of him in the ways of *peacefulness* (which his name means), and for many years he ruled Israel in peace.

One day when Solomon sat upon the throne, his mother Bathsheba came in to speak with him. He honored her by arising from the throne to meet her and bowing himself to her. Then he asked for a seat to be set beside the throne for the king's mother. So Bathsheba sat on King Solomon's right hand. The kingdom was governed in compassion, good taste, and culture, which leadership brought, among other things, exquisite community improvements and a flourishing economy.

As Solomon had been taught by his mother, he loved the Lord and kept his commandments. He made his pilgrimage to Gibeon, the high place of worship to make 1000 sacrifices before God. One night in Gibeon the Lord appeared to Solomon and said, "Ask what I shall give thee" (1 Kings 3:5).

In some of the sweetest lines of scripture, Solomon thanked God for showing his father, David, such great mercy, according as he walked before thee . . . in uprightness of heart. . . . And thou hast kept for him this great kindness, that thou hast given him a son to sit on his throne, as it is this day," said Solomon. Then Solomon admitted to the Lord that he felt needful of guidance as a new king. "Give therefore thy servant an understanding heart to judge thy people, that I may discern between good and bad: for who is able to judge this thy so great a people?" (1 Kings 3:6, 9.)

The Lord responded to Solomon. Soon his compassion and wisdom were put to good use. For example, Solomon discerned between two mothers, each claiming the same living baby as her own. Solomon asked for a sword with which to divide the baby in half: then one half would be given to one quarrelsome mother, and one half to the other. Suddenly one woman cried out to Solomon to save the child by giving the whole living baby to the other woman. Solomon judged her to be the real mother, awarding her the living baby. Solomon knew the love of a real mother. (See 1 Kings 3:16–28.)

Solomon accomplished marvelous things in his day. He established a great commercial fleet for trade with Tyre, Africa, and Arabia. He secured the sacred ark of the covenant. The Lord again visited with Solomon, who obediently built an exquisite temple according to God's specific instructions, which included details for a "molten sea" or huge metal basin of water resting on twelve carved oxen, representing the twelve tribes of Israel. Solomon's charm and his understanding heart helped him serve as a successful negotiator with neighboring countries; in these times of peace and prosperity he built magnificent edifices, gardens, bridges, and highways in addition to the temple. Instead of wars there was a stable, spiritual center in Jerusalem with but one God, who talked to their king. This unified the people.

Solomon ruled on the throne of Jerusalem for forty years. But, like his father before him, Solomon did not maintain his obedience to the Lord. He was not valiant. He began to go after false gods and heathen wives, and his kingdom was lost to him— a great tragedy for a man chosen of God.

Still, we cannot forget that because Solomon talked with God, he increased for the citizens of Jerusalem an awareness of a personal God. Some providentially were lured toward the hope of a coming Savior who would be known in his day as Jesus, the son of Mary.

Lois's Grandson

Whatever her circumstances were—a widow or perhaps a financially strapped parent who needed help from her mother while she worked outside the home—Eunice and her own mother, Lois, shared in the rearing of Timothy, whose name means "honored of God." These good people lived and moved and had their being in the time of the Great Lion of God, the Apostle Paul. They were friends with him, if not closer! The one place in the Bible where the word *grandmother* appears is in the epistle of Paul to Timothy. Lois's part in molding Timothy's character must have been significant to merit being mentioned in such a way in what has become holy writ. (See 2 Timothy 1:5.)

We don't have a record of the boy's father's name, but we know that he was a Greek married to the

Jewess Eunice, who had been converted to Christianity. This family was honored by Paul as being faithful, and he often visited them in their home. They lived in Lystra, a city in the Roman province of Galatia.

Paul loved Timothy as he would his own son. In fact, it was Paul who circumcised Timothy in the Jewish tradition when he was still a young man. The charismatic Apostle valued the unusual talents that Eunice and her mother had helped instill in Timothy. They also taught him the scriptures from his earliest days. Because the young man had so much to contribute, Paul took Timothy on many church assignments—and thoroughly enjoyed his company! Paul gave Timothy important assignments with sophisticated congregations, such as at Ephesus. There he was ordained first bishop of the church of the Ephesians.

The most honored women in the Bible are mothers—great importance is given to them. The word *mother* appears numerous times in the standard works. There are even some rare genealogical references in the Bible such as "And his mother was . . . ," significantly inferring that his mother had made a difference in the man's life or the prophet's ministry, thus explaining in a name what the person's training had been. Cultural and historical studies on the subject could be summed in the phrase, "As the mother goes, so goes society." In Ezekiel 16:44 we read, "As is the mother, so is her daughter."

A graphic symbol in the Bible is motherhood. It is the root. When Enoch looked upon the earth, he heard a voice from the very center of it, groaning, "Wo, wo is me, the mother of men; I am pained, I am weary, because of the wickedness of my children. When shall I rest, and be cleansed from the filthiness which is gone forth out of me? When will my Creator sanctify me, that I may rest, and righteousness for a season abide upon my face?" (Moses 7:48.)

Noble mothers can hasten the day!

The Madonna is the subject of many paintings of passion, but the role of mother began with Eve, whom Adam called the mother of all living. As it turned out, Eve used her agency on behalf of the rest of us by choosing the toils and briars of mortal life over lolling about in a divinely planned garden. Without the Fall, there would have been *no* children. Those who suggest women are ignored in the scriptures and parables should consider the evidence to the contrary. In the case of Timothy, credit for his quality as a servant of God is given to the grandmother Lois as well as to his mother.

Timothy had been reared so carefully by Eunice and Lois that Paul addressed him as "my dearly beloved son" (2 Timothy 1:2). Some of the wisest counsel and deepest doctrine comes to us through Paul's effective sharing of gospel principles with Timothy. For example:

"O Timothy, keep that which is committed to thy trust, avoiding profane and vain babblings" (1 Timothy 6:20).

"God hath not given us the spirit of fear; but of power, and of love, and of a sound mind" (2 Timothy 1:7).

"Let no man despise thy youth; but be thou an example of the believers, in word, in conversation, in charity, in spirit, in faith, in purity. . . . Neglect not the gift that is in thee, which was given thee by prophecy, with the laying on of the hands of the presbytery." (1 Timothy 4:12–14.)

Paul reminded Timothy that he should treat women with all purity—the elder women as mothers and the younger ones as sisters. He had come from such a home.

There is a joyous payoff to such generations of gospel training. In our day, three or four generations in a family may gather to witness a temple wedding! Extended family members crowd the airport in support for a departing young missionary who has lived worthy of the call. Youth benefit by responding to the loving care and appropriate examples of those who nurture them. Then, as with Timothy, they should remember what things of God they have learned, and of whom they have learned them.

Lucy's Joseph

In the latter days, a prophet of God presided over the Restoration of the fulness of the gospel. That prophet was Lucy's son Joseph. Sharon, Vermont, is still a placid, beautiful area of the world. Repeating mounts with slopes gentle enough to climb permit a view above and beyond lush maple trees and berry bushes. Tangled ground cover obscures a low rock wall foundation of the long gone farmhouse that belonged to Joseph Smith Sr. and Lucy Mack Smith. In the winter months the snow piles waist high all season long. So it was on 23 December 1805 when the farmhouse stood strong and firm against the cold outside and Lucy's special baby was born. Joseph Sr. and the Smith children helped in the birthing of this baby who would grow into a prophet and bring marvelous progress to the world.

Below Patriarch Peak is an obelisk signifying the birthplace of this prophet. The single shaft is made of granite and measures thirty-eight and one-half feet long, one foot representing each year of the Prophet's remarkable life. Visitors are at once impressed, voluntarily keeping voices to a whisper out of respect for this holy ground. Mary Hill, a sixteen-year-old girl at the time she wrote this poem, expressed her wonder at living in South Royalton, Vermont, just six miles west of the birthplace of the Prophet Joseph Smith:

On the Birthday of the Prophet

Rising upward, high on a hill it stands,
   exalted above all—
Rising silently, peacefully ascending
   toward our celestial home.

Rising upward—each foot for a
   year in which he lived.
Rising hand-cut, shaped, and
   polished sweetly to his memory.

Rising upward—I've seen its image
   in the glass pool beneath.
I've watched sun climb above it,
A great star coming silently through the blue
   and lighting the silver of the shaft.

Rising upward, strong as the man it honors,
   standing erect as the Prophet himself;
Rising upward, glowing strength and radiating honor,
The strength and honor of the
   prophet from Vermont.

Yet when Lucy's baby was born, so close to Christmas, no angels heralded the event with carols, no birds sang, no blossoms burst forth—the Prophet's birth was in that regard nothing like the so many gentle stories that proclaim the Savior's birth. Still it was especially exciting—a gift for the season. I'm sure the family marveled again at the miracle of a tiny infant coming forth to be a person!

"What shall we name him?" The important question at every birth.

Ideas likely flew, stirring pleasant arguments, each wanting the honor of finding the right name. But Lucy prevailed, and her suggestion surely found favor with her much-loved husband. "His name shall be Joseph, after his father!"

With that decision, an ancient prophecy was fulfilled!

When Joseph grew into a young man, he was quickly about the Lord's work, eventually receiving the metal plates engraved by selected prophets and historians of an ancient civilization. By the power of the Holy Ghost, Joseph Smith Jr. translated the reformed Egyptian language into English. Among the translated records was this stunning information: in a vision, Joseph of

Egypt saw the Nephite people in ancient America. He prophesied that in the latter days there would be raised up a prophet and seer: "And his name shall be called after me; and it shall be after the name of his father. And he shall be like unto me; for the thing, which the Lord shall bring forth by his hand, by the power of the Lord shall bring my people unto salvation." (2 Nephi 3:15.)

God had known about *their own Joseph* two thousand years ago! Lucy fulfilled Old Testament prophecy when she called her baby by that name, though she knew nothing of it at the time.

Lucy became her son's secular teacher and religious leader by guiding him in reading the scriptures and praying daily. She provided a family cocoon of faith that bolstered him against his enemies. Joseph was a responsive child, and such environment stirred him to seek God in his time of need. His custom was to withdraw himself to a private place and pray. One day when he was fourteen years old, having meditated on the text of James 1:5, Joseph went to a grove near their home in Palmyra, New York. As response to his earnest prayer, Joseph received his first vision in which he saw two beings! They identified themselves as God the Heavenly Father, and Jesus, the Son of God. This was astounding proof of two Gods, individual beings who knew Joseph by name!

Joseph Smith Jr. subsequently had numerous visions, revelations from God that sometimes included conversing with the Lord face to face. This young prophet directed the Lord's earthly affairs in opening the dispensation of the fulness of times. In orderly fashion, line upon line, the true gospel of Jesus Christ was revealed and restored to earth. After centuries of relative darkness, men could now have the fulness of the principles of salvation.

Salvation came at a high price for Lucy and her family. They all became converts to the great cause Joseph led under the Lord's guidance, but their struggles and persecutions were constant and vicious. They endured, keeping their spirits high, because each one knew that Joseph was a prophet of God and that the Book of Mormon he translated from the plates was a valid document.

Joseph's older brother Hyrum deferred to his younger brother in all things. It has been said of them: "In life they were not divided, and in death they were not separated!" (D&C 135:3.) The Smith brothers worked and served in perfect harmony. Like Moses and Aaron of old they brought much good to multitudes of people.

Eleven years before he died, Joseph gave his mother a marvelous blessing and paid her special tribute for her nurturing and courage: "Blessed also is my mother, for she is a mother in Israel and shall be a partaker with my father in all his patriarchal blessings. . . . Her soul is ever filled with benevolence and philanthropy; and notwithstanding her age, she shall yet receive strength and be comforted in the midst of her house, and thus said the Lord, she shall have eternal life."

Lucy's precious infant grew, knew, loved, served, and died as a foreordained servant of the Son of God and the Son of Mary. He is revered as the prophet of the dispensation of the fulness of times and is considered among the noble and great ones, such as Adam and Abraham. In premortal life, he developed to such spiritual stature as to become the instrument in the hands of God to restore the truth of the gospel in the last days before Jesus Christ's Second Coming. Thousands of years before his mortal birth to Lucy, prophets spoke of him by name and assignment as seer. The importance of his earthly mission was second only to that of the Savior. Joseph sealed his testimony of Jesus Christ with his blood, as a martyr. Like Jesus, Joseph died while still a young adult at the hands of satanic rioters.

The war between the forces of good and evil rages on still. Those of us who are blessed to know the whole story of the plan of happiness and to have prophets who guide us in understanding the ways and the will of God share in the glad tidings sung in prophetic truth at the birth of Jesus Christ.

Surely there is reason for a season of marvelous, joyful, exuberant, renewing celebration known as Christmas, when we mark the birth of our Savior and can remember his special servant Joseph Smith. Of Joseph, the Savior revealed, "Give heed unto all his words and commandments which he shall give unto you as he receiveth them, walking in all holiness before me; for his word ye shall receive as if from mine own mouth, in all patience and faith" (D&C 21:4–5).

Epilogue

What does all this mean to us at this season of wonder in remembering?

We believe that people are raised up in their day and time to do a task and to meet God's needs while striving to courageously meet their own mortal tests. Each person can expect to find a place in the light and service of God—not only as a reward but also as an opportunity to make a difference—inspired by Mary's Child, Jesus, the Anointed One.

Becoming familiar with the lives of ancient prophets can help lay the foundation for our current belief. Some might doubt whether anything that happened or anyone who lived thousands of years ago could be relevant to us today. But, it is! The dispensations of time, and God's children who have walked along the paths of those eras, are linked by the great truth that God is the Creator of us all. Such knowledge does not promise peace on earth among all people at all times. However, within the realm of God's plan, there is relief from the world, consolation while enduring trials, and personal growth in happiness.

There also comes great satisfaction from noting spiritual development in others in any generation who have been assisted to understand the gospel and the covenants that the Saints make with Mary's Child Jesus.

Comparing stories of the mothers and sons included in this book with people of our time, helps us recognize principles that reach across the generations.

For example, Elisabeth was barren throughout most of her long life. Only in her old age did her wonderful miracle son—John, the Baptist—come. That son grew, served God, even losing his life in his cause.

Rachel yearned after Jacob and grieved over her elder sister Leah's many sons by him. Finally she bore beloved Joseph, who she loved, trained, and enriched. He became the noble and powerful hero of Egypt. Joseph saved Jacob and his entire family from starvation. This is a fact Rachel never knew, because she died in childbirth with Benjamin, the youngest of Jacob's twelve sons.

Pharaoh's daughter—a giving, loving, foster mother to Moses—was shocked and grieved when Moses chose to negotiate the freedom of the children of Israel, leading them through the wilderness instead of continuing with her in the luxury of Pharaoh's palace. Yet, she was a leading player in God's plan to free the children of Israel—she had seen to his superb education and preparation for leadership.

Mary was chosen, submitted to the will of God, and at the cross, was assigned to be mother to another, the disciple John. She never lost her testimony that Jeshua, as she called him, is in fact the Son of God, and she his handmaiden. This she and Joseph kept in their hearts all their lives long, until the will of Heavenly Father was fully unfolded.

Though Mary and the Christ Child are the central subjects of the most majestic art, music, and literature of Christmas, and though she has been rightly called *the womb of the Lord,* Mary the person was a lonely soul. Her comfort came as ours can—only through the power of the Holy Ghost.

Because, at times, he has had no other hands or hearts to work his plan throughout the generations of time, God allows struggling people also to fulfill his purposes. We have talked of some of these valiant ones. The frightened slave girl Hagar and her son, Ishmael, fathered by Abraham, were cast out, but ultimately their descendants peopled a vast nation. It is not our genes or favored positions that make the difference in the contribution of the mother and the babe. No man, woman, child, or prophet is perfect, and God must use those he has in the ways that he needs. He enhances, blesses, and sends his angels to any willing helper in his kingdom.

Devoted mothers in our time can exult over the sacred promise for babies born in the last days. The scriptures tell us that things which never have been revealed from the foundation of the world, which have been kept even from the wise and prudent, "shall be revealed unto babes and sucklings in this, the dispensation of the fulness of times" (D&C 128:18). We are in debt to good women who nurture infants and children toward righteousness before the Lord.

Now, what do we hear in the gospel that we have received? A voice of gladness! This voice of gladness is heard today because we know Christ lives! It echoes the songs of angels who, two thousand years ago, brought "glad tidings of great joy" because Jesus was born.

We know that we have his anointed prophets among us now. We remember with gratitude the assurance that if we do what our Creator has charted for our salvation, he will bless us beyond anything we can imagine. Glory Hallelujah, indeed!

Our Lord has said, "And this is mine everlasting covenant, that when thy posterity shall embrace the truth, and look upward, then shall Zion look downward, and all the heavens shall shake with gladness, and the earth shall tremble with joy" (JST, Genesis 9:22).

There is something in the accounts of the mothers and the sons upon whom we have focused in this book that can inspire us all. As each one of us steps toward this goal of becoming more like Mary's Child, let us remember at this happy season to reach out and strengthen the children of the world. "Lo, children are an heritage of the Lord: and the fruit of the womb is his reward" (Psalm 127:3).

Bibliography

Should you want to read further concerning the Son of God and Mary, or about his disciples covered in this book, I have listed here the sources that I relied on while researching their lives.

Barrett, Ivan J. *Heroic Mormon Women*. Salt Lake City: Covenant Communications, Inc., 1991.

Deen, Edith. *All of the Women of the Bible*. New York: Harper & Row Publishers, 1955.

Durant, Will. *The Story of Civilization: Part 1 Our Oriental Heritage*. New York: Simon and Schuster, 1935.

Edersheim, Alfred. *The Life and Times of Jesus the Messiah*. Peabody, Massachusetts: Hendrickson, 1993.

Encyclopedia Americana

Encyclopedia of Mormonism

Holy Bible, King James Version

Kraeling, Emil Gottlieb Heinrich. *Rand McNally Bible Atlas*. Chicago: Rand McNally, 1956.

LDS Bible Dictionary

McConkie, Bruce R. *Mormon Doctrine*. 2d. ed. Salt Lake City: Bookcraft, 1966.

New Scofield Reference Bible. New York: Oxford University Press, 1967.

Packer, James I., Tenney, Merrill C., and White, William Jr., ed. *The Bible Almanac*. Nashville: T. Nelson, 1980.

Proctor, Scot Facer, and Proctor, Maurine Jensen, ed. *The Revised and Enhanced History of Joseph Smith By His Mother*. Salt Lake City: Bookcraft, 1996.

Protoevangelion, as translated in *The Lost Books of the Bible and the Forgotten Books of Eden*. New York: Meridian, 1963.

Rowe, Guy. *In His Image*. Oxford University Press, 1949.

Smith, Barbara B., and Thatcher, Blythe Darlyn, ed. *Heroines of the Restoration*. Salt Lake City: Bookcraft, 1997.

Webster's New Biographical Dictionary

Index